Table of Contents

How Did They Grow Up So Fast?
(A parents' guide to schools)
By Greg Tuck

Foreword

Leaving the safety and security of home to join the big wide world of school is one of the most profound journeys a child will ever undertake. Yet, while it's an exciting adventure full of joy, optimism and new frontiers, it is also full of many unknowns and fears, real and imagined, for child and parent alike.

In this book Greg Tuck has drawn upon a lifetime of experience as a teacher, leader and parent to provide a series of insightful and sensitive sign posts for the journey as parents support their child on this important first step toward independence.

The book is full of facts and wisdom, covering everything parents need to consider when selecting a school, and what to expect once they've done so. There is practical advice and a variety of perspectives provided which will be invaluable, regardless of the type and location of school chosen.

The book provides answers to questions every parent asks as they prepare themselves and their child for this important step, while also prompting other questions parents might like to further explore with their chosen school.

At its heart, this is a book that cares deeply for children as it informs choice and gives comfort on the greatest journey of all, that of learning and growing as a unique and very special person.

Greg has provided a unique and selfless service by writing a book which is in equal parts practical and philosophical. For a parent, anywhere in the world, about to send their child to school for the very first time, this book is a rich and timeless companion to have by your side.

Norm Dean
BEd. MEd.
School Support & Evaluation Officer
Council of International Schools
Melbourne,
Australia

Introduction

From the moment of birth, a human tries to make sense of the world around them. The blinding light after the womb, the sucking in of oxygen, the air around them is all new and novel but also the beginning of learning. Its senses are alive and taking in information. Its food supply has ceased. Its sense of security has gone. It bellows loudly. Instinct and genetic programming kicks in and it seeks the warmth, comfort and food from its parent. As the parent starts to hold the child, it creates a lifelong pattern of nurturing the child. The parent is the child's first teacher.

The child learns that there will be a response if it cries. The parent learns to read the signs of the child needs, be it hunger, dirty or wet nappy, colic, wind etc and reacts accordingly. As the child grows from baby through to toddler, the exploration of its environment continues at a fast pace and the parent continues to teach; guiding the child through exposure to different foods, regulating its behaviour and assisting with the reasoning process which has grown beyond cause and effect.

During those very early years, the child learns more than it probably ever will. It learns to mimic and model the behaviour of people around it. It begins the first levels of socialisation. Rules come into place and consequences are learned. Having some barriers and restrictions allows the child to, not only be safe, but also to reflect and be stimulated, not overwhelmed by what is around it. The parent plays an important role in setting those barriers and guiding the child. The time devoted exclusively by the parent to the child is not best measured in quantity, but quality. If a child is put in childcare, it doesn't stop the learning process. It is up to the parents and childcare workers to provide learning experiences for the child and to maximise those opportunities.

Exposure to regular routines and the world around them are essential elements for most children's learning. There is comfort and security in routine and there is a chance for making more sense of things in being shown new things. Without both, a child's learning may be stifled. All through those first years, so much information is being absorbed and cognitive capabilities are being challenged. Some children shy away from too much stimulation because it is overloading their capacity to learn and to rationalise what they are exposed to. This is where parents continue their teaching role and too have to make rational decisions about what is best for their child. They know their child probably better than anyone else.

However, all this seems to magically stop when the word "school" comes into play. Parents believe that they aren't really teachers despite all the education they have given their children from day one. The trained teachers at school, may know more about how to manage a group of children. They may know more about child psychology from their study, observation and experience. They may know more about teaching reading, writing and mathematics. However, they are merely taking a child who has already developed learning patterns which have been aided by the child's parents, and they are channelling that learning into specific areas. They too are the facilitators of experiences and opportunities for that child, just as the parent was. The child does not come to school as an amorphous blank canvas. It is a thinking, rational and emotional human being that has a pre-programmed capacity and willingness to learn. Many parents think that the baton has been handed on. However, the reality is that they are sharing that baton with their child's teacher. Each is equally important as the other. Each will provide opportunities for the continued learning for that child. The style of teaching, the content of what is being taught and the social environment may be different between school and home, but the importance of those learning opportunities should not be underestimated.

So, how can parents best help their child in a school situation? Possibly the first thing to do is recognise that they too are teachers. The second perhaps is to recognise that a school is just a building. They should not bring into play any fears or bad experiences that they have had as a child at school. Their child is different to them and schools have changed and continue to evolve. It may seem difficult for a child to enter into a school, but sometimes it is far more difficult for their parents to approach a school. Like most things in life, open communication is the key. Principals, teachers and parents have a great starting point for they have one thing in common and that is they want the best for the child. Each may have different expectations of how that can be achieved but if all keep that one thing in common at the forefront of their mind, their actions and their communication, the child will ultimately benefit.

The following are a series of articles that may help parents break down the mystique that seems to surround schools. For more detailed information, parents are encouraged to contact their school.

Being a Parent

It is considered one of the hardest and most taxing jobs that there is and some call it payback for being a child and the way you behaved towards your own parents. From the beginning your child depends on you, relies on you being there and meeting his/her needs. However, from a very early age children are seeking their own independence and identity. The difficulty that most parents face is the timing and the amount of independence. Each child is different. Some need more protection than others. Some need encouragement to step out into the big wide world. Wrapping them up in cotton wool is not going to give them what they need to develop and extend their minds beyond the home. Wanting them to be clones of their parents is also dubious because they will have likes and dislikes different from yours. One of the most challenging aspects for most parents is to share the care of them with others, especially strangers. Child care, kindergarten and school can often cause more anxiety for the parent than the child, who will sense the fear and trepidation of their parents and possibly mimic it.

"I want my child to be....." If the next words are happy, caring and safe, then you will be like most parents. Creating high expectations and possibly unreal ones, can be detrimental to a child. Foisting your own missed opportunities, hopes and dreams on them makes it difficult for a child to become who they want to and who they could be. Child care, kindergarten and school are opportunities for children to gain independence, to learn to fight their own battles and to find their place in the world. Unless there is a major safety issue, parents should take the time to stand back and watch their children grow, offering assistance when asked and guidance when required. Children will fall in and out of friendships and gradually acquire social skills that will allow them to mix with all sorts of different people, both child and adult.

Finding that balance between stepping in and standing back is extremely difficult. A complete hands-off approach gives the child no boundaries and thus takes away security. Constantly making decisions on a child's behalf takes away their confidence and self-belief. Parents deal with such situations in extended family situations and children learn to adapt to the different rules that are applied in different households. In multicultural societies where perhaps the rules within a family structure may be vastly different, it is the children who seem to adapt to the settings the best. In a school situation, trust between teacher and parent is very important as is the definition of the roles. Within the classroom, the teacher is in charge. Outside of school, parents are in charge. By working closely together, there can be a very smooth transition for a child. The child knows who is boss and will test boundaries for both parent and teacher. That is one way that they gain independence.

Parents don't usually have a say in who their child's teacher is and don't have much of a say in what happens within the classroom. Teachers are working with many, many children, each an individual with their own personality. Therefore, the classroom situation will always be a compromise and have general rules and practices that make a good, but not perfect learning environment. The vast majority of teachers take on board advice from parents about that parent's child. Whether that advice can be acted upon is another matter. However, the more information that teachers have about a child the better they can tailor a learning program for that child's needs. That being said, parents need to understand that the behaviour a child exhibits at home can be vastly different from what they display at school, and it has been known for parents to speak of only a child's successes and not mention the child's shortcomings.

When a child goes to school, it all comes down to trust and communication. Trust in the child that they will succeed in being happy, caring and feel safe. Trust that the teacher will provide the opportunities for a child to learn and grow and become who they are. Trust by parents in themselves that they have done a really good job before the child starts school, but that the job continues in a different form.

Choosing a School

This act seems to take up a lot of time and energy and cause a lot of stress for parents, particularly for their first child. Up until the time children go to school, parents have been responsible for much of the learning by their children. Child care and kindergarten have taken up some of the responsibility, but parents believe that they are handing over the ultimate responsibility for their child's learning to strangers and so want to make sure that these people will do the right thing by their child. Their child is a unique individual and some parents worry that their child is entering some sort of production line for the next thirteen years, and don't want to see their child lose that individuality and come out at the end as a clone of others who have entered into that process.

Children will learn in spite of the teachers, in spite of the conditions, as long as they are encouraged to learn, and they are happy. These two things are the most critical. So how can a parent make the wisest decision? Your choices may be limited by a number of factors such as distance and time taken to go to and from a school. Some schools are also zoned and unless you live in that zone, your child can't attend, although some people opt to move into a neighbourhood just because of the school.

Each school has an individuality of its own and each teacher has a range of experience, a range of talent and a range of knowledge. Teaching is an art more than a science. A teacher's job is to facilitate learning, to recognise the strengths and limitations of the students they are responsible for. What is known by teachers at the school about education, is just as important as the sharing of it with parents. The curriculum may be constant, but the delivery varies depending on the emphasis of the school, the methods used and the underlying philosophy of the school. Parents, whose last interactions with a school may have been as students, may lack the courage and indeed the belief that they can actually make a good choice. They may feel intimidated simply by the structure that they remember vividly from the time that they were in a different role. It may be hard to believe that schools have evolved in the interim, just as they have.

Talking to other parents may both help and hinder your decision making depending on the experience that parent has had with the school and what they are wanting for their child. There are some websites that rate schools but often this rating is based on testing of only academic performance. The learning of life skills is harder to assess. The achievements of individual students in their final year at secondary school is just one other piece of information. The choice of school may come down to what your understanding is of what you actually want for your child.

Does the size of the school matter? Schools are all different and the size and number of students at the school is just one consideration for parents to look at. In larger schools, a wider variety of specialist programs can be put in place and in the senior areas a wider range of subjects can be offered as precursors to university. Large schools also offer a wider choice of friendship groups for students. That being said, some large schools may seem to be more heavily structured and students may feel lost in the huge numbers of students attending. Smaller schools are often more intimate, but may not be able to provide the diversity that some students need academically and socially. From a management point of view, it is far easier to encourage parental and community involvement in smaller schools. Size is just one factor and parents need to make a choice best suited to the perceived needs of their child.

The best way to assess a school and feel confident about a decision is to actually visit the school. Schools provide all sorts of opportunities to see what they offer. These range from parent information nights, booklets and websites; however, nothing beats seeing a school in action. You can usually schedule an appointment with the principal who will explain all the best qualities of the school and who will often take you around to the classrooms and facilities that make their school stand out.

When opting for a time, the best time to see a school in action is as one of the break times is ending. You can see how the children mix with each other in a play setting. You can assess how keen they are to get back into the classroom and how quickly they settle down into what is on offer in the classrooms. You will know the right school when you walk into it and see it in action.

No school will meet one hundred percent of your child's needs. No teacher will be perfect. Your child will have a range of teachers over their thirteen years. They will undergo a range of experiences. Ongoing two-way communication with the school will help you keep abreast of what the school is trying to achieve and how well your child is going. It is important that you also provide positive feedback and ways that the school could improve.

If they are happy, secure and encouraged to learn, students will do well. If you find that the school is unable to provide those things, then it may be wise to look at other schools. Changing schools can happen. The choice ultimately is back in the hands of parents and that is where it should be. Parents know their children far better than any school can. They have begun the lifelong learning of their child well before they reach school age. Choosing a school is just another step in the process of accepting responsibility as a parent.

Managing Expectations

When parents read the glossy brochures or view the wonderful websites of schools, there is a chance that they will form an unrealistic expectation of what the school will provide for their child. After paring back all the glitz and glamour, most schools provide the same basic education. Children work in age-based classes on a central or nation-wide or state-wide curriculum. Schools provide a place of learning in a safe environment. In most cases, students will progress through the different phases of learning and gain skills and knowledge that have practical application along the way. These skills are not only academic, but also physical and social.

Each school is unique because it is made up of individuals, both teachers and students. Children will be challenged and at times the workload and the work itself may be quite difficult. In some instances, the opposite could apply. This occurs less frequently where the teachers better understand each student's limitations and capabilities. The quality of teachers does have a bearing on the outcomes for students. Small class sizes also help because they allow for greater awareness by teachers of individuals strengths and weaknesses.

Students will progress at their own rate through the curriculum presented to them. Parents expecting too much of their children may actually restrict that progress. Unrealistic pressure being brought to bear is counterproductive. The use of class averages and comparing one child with another, falls into the same category. However, if parents believe that their child isn't performing as well as they could be, then that is a time to have a conversation with the child's teacher and if necessary, the principal. There may be underlying reasons that need to be explored including whether the child can see and hear properly, is tired, unwell, bored, not understanding what is being taught, being bullied, having trouble finding friends, etc. Answers to these questions will give a common understanding between teacher and parent and agreed expectations can be put in place.

Students are normally pretty aware of their own level of skills and knowledge and where they fit in with their peers, particularly in academic and physical areas. Schools that work hard to develop the social skills area alongside the other two, are more likely to produce more rounded people at the end of the child's school life. Parents who are focused heavily on just the academic side of things may find it strange to know that employers are seeking good social skills from their employees as much as their academic ability. When students head to tertiary education and are forced to become truly independent learners, they will need all sorts of skills to cope. Their success may come down to not just their knowledge and skills, but also their ability to continue their learning on their own. Spoon feeding them all through their schooling can be quite counterproductive.

Parents need to find the right balance in terms of the expectations that they have for their child. Too low and the child will conform to those and possibly not achieve their full potential. Too high and the child will not succeed and the result will be the same. All the glitz and glamour that is displayed in a school's advertising is of little help in those situations. Teacher quality and teacher's understanding of the learning process and curriculum along with their understanding of each child's background, learning style and capabilities are what can make a real difference. Children who are keen to learn, feel safe, are happy, and know they have the support and interest of their parents don't need to have too many expectations thrust upon them. They will succeed in ways that will surprise both teacher and parents alike.

Responsibilities

There is a clear demarcation in most cases as to who is responsible for the education of children. State governments in many countries are usually the ones who provide schools, teachers and coordinate curriculum. They also set assessments across years of school for students. This allows comparison between students and also schools. This may seem as disempowering parents and perhaps also absolving them of responsibility, leaving them only to ensure that their child attends school. In all countries, parents are a vital part of their child's whole life and that includes their education. Children will achieve better outcomes if they, their parents and the school all work together on a common path.

Most schools encourage parental involvement and the better ones take on board suggestions from parents. With curriculum and assessment guidelines sometimes set outside the school by government or private bodies, there is still plenty of scope for a school to set its own agenda and create its own identity. Most schools have allocated a set amount of money to implement the priorities of these bodies, but there is also flexibility in that. Through committees and councils, parents can help set that agenda by suggesting how that money could be spent. Ultimately the school and its principal are responsible for the expenditure.

To have some influence, parents need to understand how a school functions, what limitations are placed on it and what opportunities are there to be grasped. Schools who publish policies written in clear, simple, easily understood language are doing a great service to their community. Many parents may wish to be involved in school activities and decision making, but, because of other commitments, may not be able to do so. Arming them with the knowledge of how the school functions and its aims, gives all parents a framework around which to make suggestions. Parents need to be aware that their ideas may be difficult to implement especially with competing priorities.

Ultimately the responsibility for what takes place in a school falls directly on the principal. Demands are being made from outside bodies and, when these are added to by the expectations from the broader community and parents, principals' flexibility is greatly reduced. Schools are busy places; a lot of things are happening and there is a vast range of people in them. To make them function, and function well, any positive, constructive assistance from parents is often well received. A great learning environment for students will be created and enhanced by all key players listening to each other and working together.

Parents are encouraged to:

* Read policy documents put out by the school
* See the school in action
* Volunteer for committees and councils
* Offer constructive suggestions
* Understand that the needs of their own child may not be the needs of other children
* Recognise that the principal has competing interests including those of government

Children with Disabilities

Schools are now, after more than a century of segregation, a welcome place for students with disabilities. Reason has prevailed and it is now better understood that these children have a lot to offer to society and to their fellow classmates, the least of which are the development of the idea that everyone is different, and that compassion and caring are important parts of a person's make-up. Children have better coping mechanisms than adults when it comes to dealing with people who are different. While adults try to fit in with social norms, children are encouraged to be different and explore their potential. That is what is happening with all children, including disabled.

Schools have had to adapt and cater for those students who may have a mental and/or physical disability. This is more than just providing ramps for wheelchair access and a disabled toilet. It may mean that an extra person is needed in the classroom to assist with curriculum delivery and assist a disabled child with tasks. It may mean that a separate curriculum program and expectations run side by side with a general class program. Just because a person has a mental or physical disability doesn't mean that they can't learn and haven't the right to learn, and quite importantly parents need to realise that fully abled children will not have their learning opportunities truncated because disabled children attend the same school. Indeed, in terms of civics and ethics classes, much can be gained by having all types of students in classes.

Parents can gain much from seeing a classroom in action. Classrooms are places of mixed abilities, just as society is. Observing how other children learn can allow parents to help their own children learn outside of school times. If possible, parents should take up the opportunities offered by schools to visit classrooms. If there is a disabled student in the room, much can be gained by seeing the interaction between that student and the other students.

Home and School Communication

Schools use many ways of keeping parents updated on their child's progress and activities within the school. These come in the form of newsletters, reports and the use of digital media. However, there is nothing like getting information first hand and so, wherever possible, parents are encouraged to visit the school and talk with teachers and members of the leadership team. Getting news second or third hand through a third party doesn't always convey the correct meaning.

It is just as important that opportunities exist for schools to listen and take on board, parents' praise and concerns. Having regular formal parent teacher interviews and opportunities for parents to call in and talk with teachers can create a team approach to the education of a child and quickly stop any disinformation that might exist. The dilemma for parents, apart from being confident enough to say what they would like to say, is to find the time to do it. Setting an appointment time is often the best way of doing that. Expecting teachers at the end of the day as children are being dismissed and other parents are around, to drop everything and have a long discussion doesn't always work. Often teachers have meetings and with many, many families in their grade, parents may have to wait for a suitable time. If it is critical and urgent, contacting the administration may allow the teacher to be freed up to deal with any matter of concern. In some instances where parents can't attend the school, video conferencing can be arranged.

Schools that create opportunities for parents to help in classrooms help break down barriers about what is being taught, how and why. It allows parents to work with teachers and see how their child and other children learn. There is a strict level of confidentiality expected of parents who participate. Open two-way communication is critical in a team approach to education between parents and teachers. Just as parenting is a very difficult and time-consuming job, so is teaching. Mutual respect is very important. Where a school makes contact with a parent regarding a student discipline or wellbeing issue, the outcome will most likely be more productive when a positive relationship has been previously established.

When choosing a new school or enrolling a child at a school, parents should ask what communication options there are between home and school. Education of a student doesn't happen in isolation and only in one place. Creating a relatively seamless transition between home and school creates confidence and a feeling of security in students, both of which create better learning outcomes.

Discipline

Within our society we have laws and social customs that people need to follow to allow everyone to feel safe, respected and part of society. The same applies to smaller versions of society, like families and schools. There are codes of conduct to abide by, and rewards for those who do, and consequences for those who don't. How those rules are put together is important. In many classrooms, teachers now actively involve students in framing the classroom rules. Gone hopefully are the days of the "Do not......" lists which try to cover every eventuality. In their place are simple statements about respecting others, caring of property, allowing everyone to learn, making the classroom a safe place and following instructions. Having so few, and having students involved in designing them, allows easy understanding and shared ownership of the way a classroom needs to function.

Parents need to be informed of student misbehaviour and should keep an open mind as to whether their child, in certain circumstances, would have breached these rules. What behaviour is demonstrated or accepted at home may not be the same in a school setting. Being called up to the school is very confronting for parents. Being told your child has done the wrong thing, is even more so. Sometimes the incident may be minor in comparison to any punishment and that should be calmly talked through. However, it might be a case of continued build-up of incidents. Finding the real reasons behind any failures in self-discipline is difficult, but it needs to happen.

Positive aspects of children's behaviour must also be focused on as this reinforces the rules and doesn't lead to children being labelled as bad. Their behaviour may be unacceptable, but as a person they are not. Focusing on the behaviour and not the whole person is important. Children who are continually told they are failing, be it academically or socially will struggle to improve. If the work is too difficult or too easy, then students are easily distracted. Teacher expectations need to match student capabilities or discipline issues may arise. The same applies in how the curriculum is delivered. Given that children learn best when they are doing rather than listening, better classroom outcomes can be achieved by active learning within a classroom. That is not to say that there aren't times when directed teaching should not happen.

The role of a teacher is critical in classroom management. Parents may feel that they have trouble managing the number of children they have at home, but teachers may have ten times as many. Therefore structure, self-discipline training and understanding of what is and isn't appropriate must happen for effective learning to take place. If the opportunity arises to see a classroom in action, then parents should make the most of it. Most of them are a hive of activity with students interrelating with each other and the classroom teacher facilitating learning rather than lecturing. Parents will see the need for discipline in such rooms but also witness how it is often unspoken and appears to happen naturally.

Knowing what the boundaries are helps people in general society and also helps students within the school society. Yes, those boundaries will be tested and pushed, but the fact that that they are there provides a sense of certainty and focuses students' attention on what they are at school for. These boundaries apply in both the classroom and in the school grounds, where they may be slightly different. Parents may be concerned that the boundaries are too narrow and if this is an issue then a discussion with the school principal should take place. The leadership of the school, more often than not, determines the atmosphere of the learning environment and is responsible for the welfare and discipline of children within the school. They are dealing with a large number of students from all sorts of family backgrounds and have formulated a structure that best meets the needs of all, and some compromises will have been made to try to achieve that. Good communication channels between the school, parents and students and an explanation of student expectations are critical for the smooth running of a school and lead to better student progress.

Parents can help by:

* Asking what the classroom and school rules are if they haven't been published.

* Keeping teachers informed of issues their child might be having at school or at home

* Giving feedback to your child's teacher and to the principal on all aspects of the school including discipline

* Keeping an open mind about your own child's behaviour

Community Expectations

Local communities take pride in their schools and in return have high expectations of what their school should provide. Parents have a right to expect high quality teaching to be in place for their children. They want their children to be taught the 'basics' well. They want the best teachers teaching the best curriculum in the best quality learning environment.

While parents should expect high quality from their child's school, those expectations need to be tempered with an understanding of what really can be achieved. Managing a large number of individuals, meeting all those individual's needs and implementing an ever-broadening curriculum are very challenging issues being dealt with on a daily basis. Because of such complexity, schools will never get it right all the time. They will never be able to meet or exceed the combined expectations of all the parents and the broader community. Being aware of the limitations that schools face is a good starting point for parents to have a discussion and say, "How can I help to make the educational opportunities better for all students?"

School curriculum has changed over the years. Many of the social structures within the community, including family, religious and community ones have broken down or become less important. A lot of what these offered to children in the past, including ethics and how to relate to others, are now being taught in schools. This has added extra pressure on teachers and exposed schools to criticism for not delivering the 'basics.'

Any drop in community confidence in teachers and in the standing of teachers within the community may have an impact on the outcomes for students. To deal with this successfully, many schools have an open-door policy which encourages members of the community and parents to see and sometimes participate in what takes place in schools. In doing so, these schools have helped weld together communities and now are often used as venues for community functions. Students are also encouraged gain knowledge about their own community and use their skills to help others. Choirs and other school groups visiting places such as aged care facilities, hospitals and public gatherings such as fetes and sporting events are great learning opportunities for all involved, not just the students.

To help schools provide the best curriculum and social experiences for their children, parents can:

* Support what is taking place in their child's school.

* Seek explanations from a school before publicly criticising it.

* Assist with fund raising where possible as money is in short supply in many schools

* If time permits, volunteer in any way, to assist with the heavy workload that schools are under.

* Make demands, not of the school but of the politicians who are supposed to provide schools with what they need to function.

* Be aware of what is actually taught in their child's school and the teaching methods used.

* Use outside contacts to help develop resources for the school.

* Celebrate the successes of students and the achievements of the local school

Principals, teachers and parents all want to provide the best educational experience for children. They are all seeing it from a different viewpoint. A collected combined set of expectations will see all groups pulling in the one direction and the outcomes for students improve. The latter is the most important expectation a community has of its school.

The Cost of Education

How often are people told that free education is available for students? Then comes the fine print. In many state-run systems, education is free, but because there is underfunding by governments, all the little extras add up to quite a bit. Uniforms, books, laptops, excursions, school camps and a myriad of other things seem to add up and parents have their hands in their pocket for one thing or another throughout a school year. If you have more than one child, the task becomes onerous and some families really struggle. Pride and the desire to ensure that a child doesn't miss out see many families sacrifice so much for their children.

Parents are loath to seek help from charities or contact the principal of a school because that would be an indication that they are not doing a good enough job of parenting. However, principals have access to funding through charitable entities and are discreet when it comes to who knows difficulties that are being faced. Payment plans for spreading the cost of schooling over a whole year are available in most schools. No child should be forced to miss out. Governments generally supply the building and grounds, teachers' wages and basic operational costs. Most government schools are forced to fund raise to provide extras. These fund-raising opportunities are ways that parents can support their school, meet other parents and help children in need.

Needless to say, the private schools cost a lot more in terms of fees. This doesn't necessarily make them better schools, but that is often the perception. The old adage that you only get what you pay for doesn't always apply. In most cases the curriculum is the same. The teachers in these schools have the same degrees in education, but the wages for them is paid by parents with some government assistance. However private schools are not bound to take all students regardless of financial means, academic prowess and family situation. Government schools are. A decision as to whether your child goes to a private or a government run school is a personal one.

The obligatory booklist comes out at the beginning of a school year and many families can make savings by purchasing goods themselves. There are opportunities to buy second-hand books and uniforms and parents are encouraged to donate or resell these items. While children may want brand new everything, purchasing second-hand can be a good learning experience in recycling and economics for them.

If electives are offered at a school, they will usually have an upfront cost. These are usually kept as low as possible to encourage as many students as possible to participate as often the more that do, the cheaper the cost for individuals is. The same applies to camps and excursions. If parents have concerns about the benefit of these things, they should contact the principal of their child's school. All should fit in with the curriculum that their children are learning.

When enrolling your child at a school, be aware of the hidden costs. Details are usually available on a school's website or from the administration section of the school. Find out what times of the year fees for things such as swimming programs, camps and excursions are and this will help you to budget for them over a longer period. Fee relief is usually available and students are rarely left out of activities unless they are the more expensive elective ones. Be aware if going to private schools of the overall fees and the year-by-year costs as these may fluctuate.

Education is not free, even though it is often proclaimed by politicians to be free. It is essential and it provides the platform, along with family life, for children to leap into an adult life. The gains made by education are long term. Funding such long term "projects" doesn't fit in with government election cycles and so the all-important extra funding is sought from parents. It is probably one of the best key investments that families will make as it provides social mobility for the next generation. As such, parents should explore options to get value for money. Parents should ensure that a school is contacted should money become an issue. There are ways and means to make sure children don't miss out.

Student Learning

Children in their first five years will learn more and at a faster rate than they will in the rest of their lifetime Their five senses will be more heightened than ever during that period. The rest of their lives will be based upon the foundations established in these formative years. They will learn cause and effect very quickly; a cry will usually bring then comfort, touching something hot will burn them. They will learn by mimicry, by digesting what their senses tell them and working out connections. They will see pattern and order in things around them and their brains will store and retrieve all sorts of data. The role that parents play in these years cannot be understated. Providing opportunities to experience the things around them will stimulate their brains in ways that cannot truly be measured.

Parents worry about child care and kindergarten, but these provide other learning experiences that can be taken on board by their children. School is yet another such place. By the time school comes around however that massive first rush of learning has dissipated somewhat. Children are entering a more regular pace of lifelong learning. Having more structured learning take place at schools allows for students to be able to manage the vast array of knowledge that they are becoming exposed to. Gone are the days when students were just pumped full of facts and expected to regurgitate them on demand. There is just too much information out there. Teachers provide opportunities to develop strategies to manage and use the copious amounts of information students are being exposed to.

All students will learn at a different rate and in different ways. Genetics do have influence in that, but so does the social environment that students grow up in. Schools are part of that social environment. Comparing the progress of one child with another is fraught with complications as maturity, experience, physical and mental health are other contributing factors that influence a student's capacity and opportunity to learn. Just as some children will physically grow in spurts, the same will happen with their learning. There will be light bulb moments where suddenly something makes sense, but there will also be frustrating times where learning becomes a hard slog. Children, because of their individual nature will find different subject areas easier and also more difficult to learn in. They will all have different interests too which have an impact on their ability and attitude.

Teaching is a difficult task in large groups because of the huge number of variants. The child's first "teachers" are usually their parents, who can readily identify the needs and desires of the one child and do their best to cater for him/her. In schools, the range of abilities and interests at a particular year level is enormous. Not all students' needs can be met all at once and at the same time. Some teaching practices involve steering a middle course, but ultimately that can find some students too challenged and others not challenged enough. While curriculum content has to be covered, the art of teaching involves providing activities and experiences that not only deliver the content, but foster desire for learning at all sorts of different levels.

Parents can assist and continue to be "teachers" of their children by finding out the ways that things are being taught at school, which may be far different than when they went to school. A common approach at home and school can be very enriching and supportive as the child does not have to change modes of thinking and learning continually. Schools may run parent information nights. They may encourage those parents who can, to assist in the classroom. They may publish details on line or send home information. Parents can gain a lot from these and the benefits can flow directly into their child's learning. To keep children motivated to learn is a team approach. Parents who already know and have done so much can continue to be involved in once their child goes to school. By keeping teachers informed about their child's interests, their struggles and their successes, a much more informed learning can take place that allows for the individual differences each child has.

Language Studies

There are major benefits for student learning by having them study a second language. Apart from becoming multilingual, which has its own benefits; the second language gives students a framework for an analysis of English which is one of the most complex languages to learn. Other languages have a simpler regular structure and a rhythm to them and learning one of these enhances the knowledge of the structure of English.

What parents should concern themselves with, is the language that is being taught at school and whether that language continues year after year. Chopping and changing languages, for many students, can be detrimental and they can come away with just a smattering of linguistic skills. As much as learning a language will help with understanding English, it serves little benefit if it can't be practised and used out in the wider community, for this is where the greatest gains can be made. Learning a language that won't be used beyond the school gate does not have as much merit as one that can be used in the community and when traveling to overseas places. Some parents look at the choice of language and whether it is ongoing, as one of the important criteria when they are considering which school they send their children to. Others think differently, but if learning a language is part of the curriculum, then practicality needs to be considered. English ranks only fourth behind Mandarin, Hindi and Spanish when it comes to the first languages spoken around the world. It is however, by far and away the top second language spoken. This means that in most places that children in the future will travel to, they will be understood; and, with the majority of people they will need to communicate with, they will also be understood. However, having a second language gives them an edge over those who don't have one.

One other benefit for students by having to learn another language is that they will realise how difficult it must have been for some people they may have in the past criticised, to learn English.

Homework

Homework is, for most parents, teachers and students a big bugbear. Just how much and how little depends on who you are and where you are coming from. For parents, the answer may be based on what they experienced at school and the expectations they have of their children. Different cultures have different expectations too, both of their children's work habits, the things they study and the homework they should be doing. For teachers, it can be an onerous task to set and even more onerous one to correct, or discipline those who fail to meet requirements. Few students, having done a lot of work during that day at school, want another hour or more when they get home. So, is it really necessary and is it really helpful?

A short bit of revision can be beneficial. If a child is tired, unwell or unable to concentrate; it isn't. It can set up a fight between a parent and a child that is unnecessary and counterproductive to the child's overall learning and attitude towards school. There should be no new learning involved as this may force parents into a teaching role and that changes the dynamic of the household. Teachers need to be wary to set work that can be done without parental assistance, especially as children's homelife varies. The simplest and sometimes the most valuable homework is to have an expectation that a child will read every night. The level of the text that is to be read must match what the students are capable of reading and understanding. As children are at different stages in learning how to read and interpret texts, and they all read at different speeds, the selection is very important. The one size fits all for any type of homework doesn't always work.

Understanding what a school expects in terms of homework is critical. Good communication strategies between parent and teacher will help both parties to ascertain what is expected and whether the work matches what the student is capable of. If the family is too busy, is away, the student is ill, isn't coping with the work, etc. are things that should be passed on to the teacher. These are valid reasons and will save a lot of angst for the student when the homework isn't done. Most don't want to disappoint either their parents or teachers. They will endeavour to do the impossible, but slowly gain a negative attitude to learning.

So how much assistance should parents give to their children with their homework? Ideally, if the work is not too challenging, all parents need to do is set aside some time, organise a quiet space and remove all pressure. That is not always possible because the child may not understand what parts of the homework mean. Parents explaining straight away, if possible, can turn the complex into the most simple. Sometimes, it is even difficult for parents to understand, or there may be a few meanings to it, or maybe the learning has changed since the parent went to school. In those cases, it is best to give feedback to the teacher and excuse your child from doing their homework that night, as nothing will be gained by either parent or student. Doing your child's homework is not helpful. Teachers can normally recognise someone else's handwriting, word usage and level of thinking. Besides, doing it may see your child being set more difficult homework and that isn't helpful.

The length of time spent on homework should vary according to the student's age, their level of learning and their home situation. For some young students, reading and/or being read too is enough. As they get older, counting patterns, tables and some simple research can be added. Parents and teachers need to bear in mind that students have been at school for over seven hours, so adding hours of extra work on top of that, won't achieve as much as they think. Students may have different teachers and these teachers need to communicate with each other so that homework tasks they set don't overlap and demand extra time from students. Some schools are setting homework and assignment tasks across weeks and months so that students are not overburdened and can plan around family activities and outside school interests.

Having a common understanding of what homework is to be done, the reason for it and the expectation of it being done should make the task less burdensome. Allied with feedback opportunities for students, parents and teachers, homework can be quite valuable.

Digital Education

The advent of massive changes in digital technology may seem overpowering to many, but this is the world students are growing up in and curriculum at schools needs to reflect that. From very early ages, children are becoming very adept at using it. They do not have the inbuilt fear of some parents who are reluctant to use it because they think they might do something wrong. Making a mistake is a learning opportunity. Children will find short-cuts and quickly outpace many adults with what they can do. That alone should be celebrated.

There is quite rightly a concern that too much screen time is a bad thing. In a classroom situation, teachers use technology as a tool for learning. However, they realise that is not the only tool, and expectations are set so that children are to have other non-digital ways of learning similar things. Access to the internet has opened doors to what are essentially millions of books in thousands of libraries. It has also allowed them to communicate and share ideas with students across the world. Instead of being force fed a series of facts and expected to regurgitate them, students are taught skills on how to research information, collate it, filter it, question it and respond to it.

The skill of reading and promotion of books is still a core part of the curriculum. Indeed, the setting up of a regular reading time is encouraged. Somehow the feel and texture of a book adds more reality to the message contained inside. This applies across a whole lot of fields because an image on a screen can't replicate the real thing. Many students are tactile learners and need to feel real things to gain a greater understanding. People have been concerned that children won't see the difference between reality and a digitally manipulated reality. However, the hardest critics of digital technology are the ones who use it the most. Students are taught to creatively make and manipulate images and that gives them a greater understanding of what they are actually seeing on the screen.

Very little 'coding' work needs to be taught as programs are very user friendly. The use of video interfaces has allowed students to work on common projects between classrooms and all across the world. They share understandings, skills and ideas with others which broaden their own knowledge. Parents and schools have also found this to be very useful way of communicating with each other in today's very busy world.

Monitoring the use of technology and how long students spend on it takes place within schools and parents similarly do it at home. Cultural or economic reasons may prevent the use of technology at home so parents who do not have the same technology available at home as that used in schools should approach the school. Their children should not be disadvantaged by not having the resources at home. Nor should they be singled out because of it.

Parents can greatly assist their children by:

* Setting appropriate screen time at home.

* Setting strict guidelines when students go on-line.

* Ensure that proper ways of using the internet are practised and that cyber bullying is reported.

* Being aware that minimum age requirements for most social media platforms is thirteen.

* Becoming aware of the digital technology policies and practices within the school

* Upskilling themselves in digital technology. (Sometimes children are the best teachers)

* Informing the school of the technology limitations at home

* Monitoring what their children are using the technology for

* Encouraging non-screen time being used effectively, especially in outside activities in the arts and sport.

Reading

For some children the decoding of the hieroglyphs on a page is very confronting and for some, it is a breeze. Students learn at different rates and at different ages. Reading is a very complex function for the brain to handle. If you think about it, the eye (or in the case of a blind person reading braille, the fingers), have to focus on what appear meaningless individual images, then the brain has to decipher what they stand for, how they link with other images to make up things called words, which also represent other things. These words are linked to form sentences which then have some meaning that a person can relate to. Each one of these processes, and the sub-processes associated with them, have to be learnt. For most children, even before they get to school, they have many of these things already in place. A school's reading curriculum is there to plug the gaps and to extend the breadth and depth of the meaning behind the words.

Parents have already done a lot of the teaching of reading. They have surrounded their children with books. They have read to their children and thus they have modelled the processes involved. They have shown that text has meaning. They have shown that text is read from left to right, that pictures give contextual clues as to what the text means. They have exposed children to a wide variety of writing styles. They may not have taught phonics as a strategy, but the sound that they produce as they read gives children clues as to what letters and groups of letters sound like. Young children pick up on these things. They quickly learn familiar repeated words. Take the word 'the.' It is very common, but phonetically it doesn't work. Children take it on board because they see it so often. It may confuse them when they see it inside the words, 'them', 'they' and 'others,' but they quickly take on board that things are different.

English is a very complicated language and a wide variety of strategies are used to read it. Simply teaching phonics alone doesn't work. Good readers who come across a word they don't know, will often substitute a word that makes sense instead, rather than stop the flow of what they are reading. Reading is all about making sense of what is written. By continually stopping to sound out a word means that for some, the sense is lost.

Some of the strategies that work are:

* Using pictures to give clues as to what the text is about

* Rereading a passage if it doesn't make sense

* Substituting a word that makes it make sense. (Correcting it can happen later)

* Not relying on phonics as the sole way of working out what a word is

* Predicting what is about to happen

Parents often wonder:

* Should I tell my child what the word is?

Yes, if sense is being lost. But it isn't the first strategy to use as that won't encourage independence in reading.

* Is my child okay to have their finger follow the words?

Yes, as some children have difficulty focusing on which line that they are reading. However, over reliance will slow the pace of reading.

* What do I do if the book seems too hard?

If it is something that your child is really interested in, share the reading with him or her. Perhaps even read it to your child first and then have them read it. If it is a book that the school has sent home and is too difficult, let the teacher know.

* If the book is too easy, what then?

Sometimes children and adults like to read just for pleasure. A book doesn't have to be challenging all the time.

* What if my child just doesn't want to read?

There will be situations where this will happen as it does for adults. Perhaps the book is boring, too hard, too easy. Reading is essential but must also be enjoyable. Parents are in the best situation to assess the mood of their child and to determine why there is no desire to read. Share what you know with your child's teacher.

* My child would prefer to spend time on the computer than read. What do I do?

While there is a lot of reading done on computers, it is only one medium. Your child needs to read in a whole lot of different contexts from newspapers, magazines, street signs, even displays in supermarkets. Books are another essential medium and an expectation needs to be set that these should also be read.

Parents can assist their children in a number of ways. The best few are to ensure:

* That the books that their children are reading are of interest to them.

* That the text is at a level they can understand without sense being lost.

* That a regular reading habit is established

* That they don't compare their child's performance with other siblings or children in the classroom

* That they continue to model reading even after school has 'taken over' the responsibility for teaching reading.

* That they communicate regularly with their child's teacher about types of books and strategies they see their child using.

Mathematics

Imagine how difficult it is for a child starting school. They are instantly confronted with not one, but two languages to learn. Even though it is far more complicated, one is more familiar and they have been exposed to it from an early age and use it every day. They are confronted with yet another that has fewer symbols and is far more logical, but in the past has been taught without many strategies and little context. It is the lack of context that puts children off because a mathematician's shorthand on its own is hard to understand. Many find it frustrating and their eyes glaze over when maths is being taught. They go home and perhaps their parents say, "I was never very good at maths" and that just reinforces what they think. It is all too hard.

Yet people's brains are wired to see patterns, to make logical connections and to remember. Maths is all about making sense of symbols, learning what they represent and manipulating them to gain a better understanding of what is around them. In a way it is like learning to read. The teaching of mathematics has changed a lot over the years and more emphasis is being placed on understanding than on just rote learning.

Students still need a tool bag of facts and strategies for the task. Number facts and tables are still relevant and need to be learned. Having these allows students to work faster through more complex ideas. Many children already have an understanding of number and a lot of mathematical concepts before they reach school. They can see patterns, count, have a simple understanding of money and measurement and can sort things into categories. It is the grasping of what the symbols mean and can do, that is the tricky bit. It gets far more complex when suddenly the alphabet is dropped into the mix in what was known as algebra. Again, context is the key to keeping students motivated. Schools that are able to get their students to make these real-life connections have greater success.

Children from an early age need to learn to estimate and then check. Whether it be measuring how long something is, how much something weighs or how much a certain time period is; estimating helps build concepts that they will come to rely on. Estimating using numbers should be a positive experience. For too long mathematics has been seen as having only right and wrong answers. Whereas in daily life, adults use close approximations all the time, as exactness isn't required very often. A student may have got the mathematics correct but the arithmetic incorrect. The whole of their logic shouldn't be dismissed with a huge red mark placed over it as this risks a negative attitude towards mathematics.

Fractions need not be seen as difficult either because we use them all the time when we talk about time, when we measure things etc. It is when they are treated abstractly then students have difficulty. Having a visual image or a real-life example makes the learning lock into place. The use of percentages, decimals and vulgar fractions should be interwoven as children see these all around them. By separating them from each other and from real situations, we are actually making it harder for children to understand.

Understanding large numbers is not difficult for young children but there has been a tendency to limit their learning of these. Children quickly learn that a number is determined by what digits are in what place. They recognise patterns so when they learn that 2+2=4 why not expand that to 20+20=40 or 2000+2000=4000? Think how much confidence will grow from an understanding of that.

Mathematics is not hard. We have made it seem that way by not building on what children already know; by treating it as a separate entity, if you like, a whole new language to master and by taking it out of real-life situations. Children are surrounded by number and maths very early on in life. Their mind makes sense of things very quickly and most enjoy a challenge. There are different levels of learning that take place. A simple conversation about a sign on the side of the road that has a sixty in a circle can lead to so much. A young child may ask what it says. An older one may ask what it means and here you can discuss speed time and distance. At a higher level that discussion leads to the fact that speed and time have an inverse relationship. The faster you go the less time it takes. You will know that you have achieved success when a child points out that at a certain speed it will take longer as you will be pulled over by the police for speeding.

As a parent, you can help by:

* Helping children see patterns and links in real life situations

* Playing logical games with them

* Providing measurement activities

* Encouraging the learning of number facts and times tables

* Remembering that children will progress at different rates in the different areas of mathematics. Some may take longer to make the connections than others.

* Being positive about their learning

The Arts

To provide a balanced well-rounded education, children need exposure to the Arts including: drama, dance, visual art and music. Given that some students will end up in the Arts and entertainment industry, these should not be treated as add-on subjects. Some children will actually be quite talented in these areas and that may be the source of their major success and enjoyment within the school system. Often in schools, where time or financial constraints are a concern, the Arts can be an area where cuts happen. Good quality staffing in these areas can also be a problem. This has tended to make the learning of the Arts seem of lesser importance to parents and students.

Drama is an area that strengthens the teaching of English, particularly in listening, speaking and reading. It also has great relevance to writing, grammar and punctuation as it places these in context, where the correct phrasing, intonation and understanding of the power of words are seen by students.

Music and mathematics may seem to have little to do with each other, but there is a very strong link between the two as most music is mathematically based. They may have different ways of notation, but there is pattern and order, understanding of fractions and algebra that exists within both.

Dance also involves repeated patterns, but added to it is spatial and body awareness. It can be as physically demanding as any physical sport and is seen by experts as being a valuable addition to improving a person's strength, physique and concentration.

Not all students are abstract thinkers, some need to visualise and draw what they see. Drawing, painting, sculpting are excellent ways that students have of expressing themselves, more than just in words. Parents usually praise their children's first art work, but as these children grow, the praise diminishes and criticism of technique and of the final image takes its place. Students then walk away from visual art because they haven't got the skills to produce the work to a standard that meets their increased expectations and those of others. Creativity is lost to conformity, closing down one valuable area of expression. A positive approach from parents and teachers can change that.

During the early years of schooling, the Arts are interwoven within other subject areas and they complement all subjects, broadening understanding, giving opportunities for some students to shine, and allowing learning to be seen in different contexts and forms. For some students, the Arts is also seen as a break from the hard slog of learning English and Maths, and allows them to still be learning, yet come back refreshed to tackle these difficult more time-consuming areas.

We want our children to come out as balanced, content and socially well-rounded students. The Arts, taught well, greatly assists in that, especially with the development of social skills. They take the student away from their desks and encourage them to interact with others within a learning environment. To assess a child's progress by just looking at a single dance routine or a portfolio of paintings and drawings, or even just listening to a small role in a play or their first attempts with a musical instrument, does not take into account what has been gained in other areas and in social skills through the participation in the Arts program. It helps them to become confident and to experiment. These are huge benefits in the overall scheme of things.

Not every child will become a Michelangelo, a Nureyev, a Maria Callas or a Cate Blanchett. Learning the Arts is not all about that. It is a place for expressing ideas in different forms. It is a time for becoming more self-aware. Parents should continue to encourage their children to participate in the various forms available, either at home, privately or at school. Many schools welcome outside artists and parents to work with children. Parents whose time, confidence and talent permit, should consider offering their expertise.

Science and Technology

Science and technology have become increasingly important in today's modern world. In the past they have had the reputation of being very boring dry areas of study and that students needed to be extremely intelligent to understand what was being taught. However, there is such a diverse range of fields within the broad area of science and technology, that interested students of varying abilities can make very good progress. Students who are creative, logical and persistent or combinations of these will succeed. A school's role and teacher's role is to create and foster interest among students. This no longer takes the form of pumping them full of facts, but giving them open ended hands-on activities, often based on a problem. Skills are taught to help students develop a possible solution to the problem. They learn to form a hypothesis, experiment, record results and then use those results for further investigation. By asking questions rather than giving answers, teachers encourage students to examine the world around them.

Trial and error experimentation has begun well before children walk through the school gate. Parents already have experienced the overt "why" phase children go through. That questioning doesn't stop as children become more articulate and independent. Good teachers harness that inquisitiveness and provide a structured environment and approach to assist children to find out the answers. Parents have often done similar things by allowing children to experiment and discover for themselves things they are interested in. Providing opportunities rather than answers, helps to build a scientific kind of thinking.

Science and technology have often been seen as the realm of males, but there is no reason why it should be. Inquisitiveness doesn't belong to one gender; past social norms have merely dictated it that way. As the world becomes more reliant on science and technology, there will be an increasing number of jobs that will become available in these areas. By making science and technology gender neutral, schools are not closing off interest and potential careers for half of their students.

Parents can also encourage their children to continue with the study of science by creating opportunities for them to experiment and build on existing knowledge. Doing research rather than just hearing answers, stimulates an active mind. Providing toys and equipment that assist in getting children to ask "why?" and "what if...?" helps to develop a scientific approach for children. Children will want to test limits and parents can help them to design ways of testing their theories safely. As in most other subjects taught in schools, parents don't need to know all the answers to help their children. They just need to be able to guide them into how to find out what the answers may be.

Schools should have a science and technology program running, either as part of the general curriculum taught in primary classrooms, or as separate subjects throughout the entire primary and secondary years. The body of knowledge and skills continue to grow and that is why towards the end of secondary school, subjects are broken into specific fields even though they are still linked. Peer pressure, lack of success and community norms can see many students decide that science is not for them. Good quality teaching and innovative curriculum throughout a child's time at school can boost retention rates in science and technology and allow students to have broader pathways into careers.

The asking of why when it comes to the world around them, doesn't stop as students get older. Many students are searching for answers and having a good working knowledge of science and technology, its background, applications and how to use it, will assist their understanding of that world.

Speaking and Listening

Articulate children who can converse with each other and with adults are what we want and schools provide opportunities for them to develop those skills. Of speaking and listening, listening is probably the most important skill. To be able to understand what another person is saying, whether you agree with them or not, allows proper dialogue to take place. Being able to state clearly your own point of view confidently is important throughout life.

Children learn to speak by listening and interpreting others. Parents have done most of the hard work before children reach school. Schools merely refine and extend speech patterns, provide opportunities for students to speak at various levels, and to give them structure and tools to mount persuasive arguments on a variety of topics.

The nature of each individual child is vastly different. Some are shy, some are voluble, some prefer to speak rather than listen. Within our social structures, speech patterns vary. What you say to your close friends is often different in tone and message to how you address family members, people in authority or those of different ages and backgrounds. The important element is that you get your message across in a way that the receiver of that message will understand and take on board. Parents have modelled this for their children and also given their children experiences in different situations before their children even walk through the school gate for the first time. Children are very quick to pick up social cues and their framework for how, when and what they should say and why are generally in place but not locked in during their early years.

Parents can assist their child's development by reminding them of appropriate language, using words to clearly explain what it is they want. Enunciation and clarity of speech modelled to them does make a difference from an early age. Picking the right tone and listening before speaking are aspects that most parents encourage as part of their children's upbringing. Should you believe your child needs speech therapy, contact the school as soon as possible as most schools have links with speech therapists who can quickly assess and provide activities that improve speech. As speech is highly dependent on hearing, the same applies should your child have auditory problems. These may already have been picked up much earlier so, on enrolment of your child at a school, inform the school of the progress being made and ensure that as your child progresses that their teachers are kept informed.

Formal speaking opportunities are provided by schools and a number of students find these daunting. Having a good knowledge of the subject matter, self-belief and practice beforehand are ways that students can get through what they may believe is an ordeal. Positive encouragement from parents is extremely valuable in these situations.

As children develop and gain independence, they will become more argumentative, more assertive and use inappropriate language. This is normal. However, if good speaking and listening strategies have been put in place from an early age, then the road may be less bumpy than otherwise.

The ability to both speak and hear used to be associated with a person's mental capacity. Time and a greater awareness have taught us that is not so. Sometimes those who listen far more than they speak are the wisest as they are taking on board what is being said, thinking things through and then say concisely and clearly what their thoughts are.

As adults, we tend to communicate more through speaking than any other means. Assisting your child's speech patterns and giving them an understanding of social expectations and circumstances of speech will help them immensely.

Writing

Many years ago, handwriting was seen to be far more important than the writing that is done to express yourself on paper, or these days on screen. Handwriting is still a skill that needs to be taught, but the ability to organise your thoughts and communicate these using the written word is much more valuable. Students are still assessed on their ability to write clearly and concisely and this can be in a digital format or a handwritten format.

Children are exposed to printed material very early in their lives and understand that books, words and letters convey meaning. They begin early to express their own thoughts in a written context, often with scrawled letters and pictures. As their exposure to printed text grows and their speech patterns form, what they are able to produce changes from barely recognisable letters to readable words. Encouragement and modelling from parents see the quick development and many children can write letters, their name and some words before they get to school. Some can't despite the best efforts of their parents, but as all students learn at different rates, parents shouldn't consider their child or themselves as failures.

Continually correcting a student's work because of poor grammar, incorrect spelling or lack of neat handwriting can be counterproductive towards progress in writing, for this focuses more on these aspects than the message that is trying to be conveyed. Incidental and positively delivered corrections will not have that effect. The question then arises, whether children should be taught to spell and the answer is yes. Just as children may struggle over words when they read and lose the meaning of the text; children need to know that people will not understand the meaning of their work if the reader spends too much time deciphering words. This even applies if they are using a digital device to write as the spelling and grammar checker won't resolve all issues without the person having a good knowledge of spelling and grammar.

There are various forms of writing used in a variety of contexts. As adults, the sort of writing style for a shopping list is different from that used for a job application. Students will gradually learn and practice different styles or genres beyond the narrative they usually begin with. They will use writing to outline arguments, complete surveys, write letters and journals and as part of almost every subject they cover in school. Parents can assist by extending the range of books that they read beyond just stories. Reading a newspaper, magazine articles, instruction manuals, recipes etc will expose children to different writing styles and children will see that writing comes in different forms that they can imitate.

Some students will write for pure enjoyment, others will write if there is a purpose and there will be a group that do it for both reasons. Being hypercritical of what is produced can be damaging to improvement. Rather than dismiss the whole piece of work, parts of it should be highlighted and given praise and perhaps one or two constructive suggestions put forward. A lot of time, work and thought usually goes into a piece of writing, particularly for those to whom it doesn't come naturally. To not acknowledge that, nor recognise the message that the writer is trying to convey may be seen as a personal attack.

Organising thoughts, planning a piece of work and working out who the audience is, are three important steps that usually are necessary for a good piece of work to be produced. This happens automatically for many adults on simple but still important pieces of work such as shopping lists. To write an essay, a poem, a persuasive text or even a narrative, students need to understand the usual format and plan before they put pen to paper. Schools are teaching these forms of writing, building on skills learnt earlier. There is still an expectation that a first draft will be edited by the student which includes them checking spelling, punctuation and grammar to the best of their ability. It is during the rereading of the text that correction takes place as the first phase of writing involves putting down the thoughts and messages that are to be conveyed.

Finding out what a school's approach is to writing is an important thing for parents to do. Knowing this, parents can help at home with some of the elements such as spelling, grammar, punctuation and formatting. However, the best things that parents can do are:

* being positive about efforts produced
* being aware of the importance and purpose of the piece
* being constructive when offering a critical opinion
* ensuring that any judgements of it made are in line of the learning age of the child.

Sport and Physical Education

Academic and social education form only parts of what is necessary to help produce a well-rounded student. Sport and physical education are important aspects that form part of the curriculum. A student's fitness and understanding of their body and what it can do are taught within the school framework. As children develop and grow, they need to understand what the strengths and limitations are of their body. This does not mean that they are all being taught to be champion athletes, but the awareness of themselves as physical beings has huge spin offs in other areas.

The opportunity to work in team situations both within the classroom and outside the classroom encourages them to see what they and others are capable of. The individual differences can be more pronounced in sport and physical education and teachers need to be aware that some children may have more ability than others. The management of curriculum in these areas is critical as it needs to match an individual's attributes. Physical wellbeing is important and the teaching provided should focus on what success can be achieved not constantly on their failures. This can turn students away very quickly. Parents can assist by ensuring that teachers are kept informed of any illness, reluctance to participate or any disability their child has. They can also assist by not focusing on the winners' and losers' side of sport.

There is a sense of belonging that comes with being in a team situation. There is a connection that can be forged because everyone within a team has a role to play and are all trying to achieve the same goal. These connections can be the beginning of lifelong friendships. In some situations, school provides the only opportunities for physical exercise a child may have. Simple skills such as throwing, catching, running and the use of foot skills do not always come naturally and easily for students. Developing an awareness of how what they eat and drink affect their health is part of the curriculum taught. The effects of drugs, along with sex education, and how their body functions are not always taught at home. Schools provide a structured program over a number of years to teach students these as they both physically and mentally mature. In some countries, however, schools have been restricted from teaching some aspects as they are seen as a parent's or a cultural responsibility.

A growing understanding that everyone has different strengths and weaknesses, along with an awareness of the physicality of their own body are very important for students to learn. The application of this knowledge in team situations will better prepare them for working with others in society in many different roles and experiences.

Excursions and Camps

Education is not confined to a small classroom or internet connected screens. Hands on activities outside of the school help solidify understandings. Children need to view the world through their own eyes and not the filtered eyes of someone who has seen it and merely talks about it. The mere fact that they are going somewhere special to observe something or participate in something imprints those things on their memories. To do so with their friends and classmates adds to the retention.

Excursions are an important part of the learning program at school and, although they are expensive for many families, the rewards are high. Schools should give advance warning of excursions and these excursions should be tied to the curriculum being taught and not be just a one-off fortunate opportunity. They should also realise that they come with an impost on families and make arrangements so that no child misses out. The fact that some children will have been to the venue before may put some parents off, but visiting with other students is a totally different experience than visiting it with a family.

The same can be said for school camps where students are taken out of their normal routine and setting and while participating in different activities also are expected to assist in the running of the camp. This helps them develop independence, better social skills and a greater awareness of themselves and others. Camps take different forms. Some are set in bushland; some are in major cities and others can be even overseas. The length of time away from home is determined by their ability to cope in a situation. For young students it might be just a sleepover in their own school. For older students it may be for as long as two weeks, especially if international travel is involved. Camps are expensive and parents should seek assistance via the school principal if money is an issue. Often there are kind benefactors who can be found or grants that can be accessed that will subsidise the cost. Money should not restrict students' attendance at these programs.

In some countries, excursions and camps are arranged of a service nature, where students will spend a week or so helping a community with a particular need. Usually these are very practical experiences where students might build a school, set up water wells, paint & refurbished village schools, help in orphanages etc. these promote an awareness of civic responsibilities and allow students to see how other people live.

Parents may be reluctant for their child to go on camps and excursions and the reasons may be manifold. There may be cultural, religious or health reasons and these are all valid. It is up to the school to explain what benefits are available to students from attending and then it is for the parents to decide. An early decision helps the school to plan.

For teachers, many of whom would feel more comfortable teaching back in their classroom, excursions and camps can be very taxing but also enlightening as they see their students in a totally different light. Camps are especially difficult as there is no downtime for teachers as they are responsible for their students twenty-four hours a day. They aren't paid any more for the time, stress and care involved. They are away from their own families for that time as well, so parents need to be aware of the sacrifices that teachers going on a camp are making.

In years to come, students will remember their experiences and what they learned on camps and excursions, possibly far more than what was taught in the classroom. They will form friendships that may last a long time. These activities reinforce their academic learning but add so much to their social skills and personal understanding at the same time. For these reasons alone, parents should consider encouraging children to attend if at all possible.

Religion in Schools

In many countries, religion forms the backbone in the school system and apart from academic education, time is spent learning the main elements of a particular religion and the culture that it is incorporated within. There are countries which do not allow religion to be taught in schools at all. Finally, in other countries, religion is taught in schools that parents specifically enrol their children in. Other schools within that country are secular in nature but generally teach an ethics component to their students. This last group of countries gives parents choices. They allow parents to make decisions on behalf of their children. Many of these countries are multicultural and have a range of religions for parents to choose from.

Basically, the government run schools are usually secular and parents have to go to privately run schools for religious teaching to be taught during school hours.

Many of these government run schools have an opt-in component that allows children to be taught basic religious beliefs during the school year in times when ethics classes are taught. Parents need to familiarise themselves with the options that are available to them if religion is an important part of what they would like their children to learn. The same applies should they prefer not to have religion taught to their children. Discussing with a principal what a school offers regarding religion is advisable prior to enrolment.

Friendship Groups

When beginning school or changing schools, parents are quite rightly concerned about their child being able to establish new friendship groups. Children are usually very resilient, but also very aware of the people around them. They will soon find people that they will like and get on well with. For some children this may take some time. Being with a group of children of around the same age is helpful as often common interests can be shared. Working together within the classroom and during sporting activities provides students with focused opportunities to work as a team on a common project. They learn how to understand, communicate and adapt to other people.

There will be clashes of personality. Friends will be gained and lost. Small cliques will exist within schools. These are merely a reflection of what happens in society and students learn social skills that enable to adapt to these situations. However, parents need to be aware of bullying that may be taking place. Discreet conversations between parents, teachers and principals can quickly quell such activity. Bullying can take many forms, from physical and verbal aggression through to isolation and rejection. Being aware of your child's change in behaviour and their discomfort is important. Acting on it by contacting the school calmly and quietly is also very important. Bullying is not a one-off event and bullies normally don't have one victim. If it happens going to and from school or at school, the school should be the one to deal with it.

Friendships that are forged at school are often the ones that people keep throughout their lives. Parents may think that their child may not be the best judge of who their friends should be. However, interfering in the process of choosing friends can be counterproductive. Parents will find that if their child has been able to gain a good set of ethics and social skills, has an awareness of themselves as an individual, and has a range of opportunities to find friends, they will in all probability choose very wisely in the long term.

Non-school Times

The time that students are not at school can be used valuably in many ways. One of the best ways is as a break from the work they have been doing. During school terms, students with minds and bodies still growing, tire quite easily. After a full school day, they need a break. After a full school week, their body and mind need to do something different. These things actually help focus their learning rather than detracting from it. Doing non-school activities doesn't mean they stop learning because learning takes many forms. The skills and knowledge they gather outside of school hours help them to become more well-rounded individuals and by being in different situations, they gain new experiences.

Students going on family holidays during school terms do not need to be saddled with a lot of school work to complete. Often the richness of what they see and do keeps their minds alert and allows a different sort of learning to take place. The keeping of a diary during their holiday is often more than enough. Copious amounts of worksheets or digital activities are not as mentally stimulating as exploring new experiences.

Children who have been trapped within the four walls of a classroom often need to have some physical activity after school or on weekends. Joining sporting clubs, going to playgrounds or just playing with friends is not only an essential healthy and worthwhile thing, it helps them to develop social skills that will stand them in good stead back in school and in later life.

If homework set by their teachers has to be completed, better results are obtained by having a break after school and then completing it. They come back refreshed and are able to do it easier and faster. Getting the right sort of balance is very important. Too many hours of study can affect student performance and what is hoped can be gained can be lost entirely. Parents are very aware of their children's capacity to complete tasks. They know when their child is tired, unwell and not able to focus.

Out of school hours they are the ones who set the agenda. Teachers are usually not fully aware of each family's situation and also of the ongoing needs of the child. Out of school times, students are still learning. It doesn't have to be just academic work set by a school. There is so much to learn about life than just that.

Reports and Parent/Teacher Interviews

If your child's school has set up good two-way communication avenues and you have made use of them, just how well your child is doing both academically and socially, should not come as a surprise to you in their reports and in parent/teacher interviews. Ongoing feedback by parents and teachers, means that action can be taken early to improve children's learning and if necessary, behaviour. Reports are just formal statements of progress made, but should also include strategies to try for the next period of time, otherwise they offer little more than a starting point with no intended destination or method of getting there.

There is no getting around it, many teachers find written reports difficult to write and would rather discuss face to face with parents what progress has been made. They are often written in isolation without knowing much about the family background, which may have a lot of bearing on progress at school. Ideally, they are merely a starting point for a conversation such as held in a parent/teacher interview.

One important purpose of reports and interviews is to share knowledge and plan strategies together. However, groundwork needs to be laid to make the best of the opportunities. As a general rule, teachers rarely get feedback and tend to be defensive of what teaching has occurred. It doesn't help if parents arrive at interviews demanding to know why their child isn't performing up to their expectations. If there has been positive communication before the formal interviews, then such situations rarely arise.

Should students attend the interviews? In most cases, it is a good idea. After all, it is about them. They will receive the message that their parents and their teachers are working together and have a good idea of progress made and why. Students are also able to contribute and explain their point of view and this just adds to the body of knowledge that builds future strategies. The success of these three-way discussions is entirely dependent on the attitudes that all three bring into the interview.

The older they are, often the more embarrassed by their parents many students will feel. This needs to be recognised and allowed for.

It all comes down to communication. Teachers need to realise that for many parents, being called up to the school, causes a lot of anxiety. Even a note from a child's teacher can cause stress. Therefore, schools need to look at how they celebrate the positive achievements of students and inform parents of the positive aspects of the learning that is happening. They also need to recognise that some parents may not have the time or skills to help their child, and as a consequence, offer assistance if possible. Just because a parent can't get to a parent teacher interview doesn't mean that they are not interested in how their child is progressing. It is difficult for many parents to get to parent teacher interviews let alone see their child's classroom in action or assist in the classroom. Flexible arrangements can be put in place and parents who are having difficulty should contact their child's school.

Always there seems to be some confusion about the marking system that is being used to monitor progress e.g. what does a C actually mean? Are students rated against each other, against national standards, against their potential? How are these assessments made? Are they based on tests, on classroom work, on teacher judgements? The answers vary from school to school. It is incumbent on schools to explain in layperson's terms just what the report actually means or it becomes just a worthless piece of paper and not a building block for further progress. If parents don't understand, then it is important that they seek clarification, or they will miss the opportunity to help.

Being involved in your child's education involves good two-way communication and opportunities for that to happen. Make the most of the opportunities you get and you will get an insight into how your child is progressing academically and socially. You may also see a different side of them that you hadn't expected and one worth celebrating.

School Uniforms

The arguments about wearing school uniforms are both complementary and contradictory and most schools have come down on the side of the wearing of them. Indeed, that is one of the conditions of enrolment in many schools.

The wearing of a uniform promotes a stronger bonding with a school, even if just visually. Students are more readily identifiable as belonging to a certain group within the community. However, in a school environment that is supposed to promote and cater for individuality, it is hard to reconcile such uniformity, unless the wearing of a uniform takes clothing out of play and allows people to focus on the person underneath. Visitors to schools are confronted with a mass of students all looking pretty much the same and therefore they have to look harder to see the individual. This actually highlights individual differences.

What wearing a uniform does is to remove one aspect of the social disparity that exists economically between the rich and poor in the school environment. There are no fashion parades, no designer clothes, no keeping up with the latest fashion trends; all of which put an unneeded pressure on family finances. Various charities will also assist with the purchase of school uniforms for those in need.

Uniforms are usually designed to be hard wearing and because bulk quantities are going to be purchased, are often cheaper to purchase. With children growing so quickly, there is often a high turnover of items and these can be recycled through second hand shops within a school.

The wearing of school uniforms on excursions, particularly to crowded places assists teachers in keeping track of their charges and should a student become lost, makes them easier to find.

Some schools have very strict rules when it comes to the wearing of uniforms. Unfortunately, this puts the onus on the child where in many cases it is undeserved. Parents can assist simply by sending a note or calling their child's school in advance to explain.

Parents may wish to have their child stand out and their individual differences catered for, but uniforms do not prevent that. They are worn for other reasons and students are assessed on who they are and not what they wear.

www.ingramcontent.com/pod-product-compliance
Lightning Source LLC
Chambersburg PA
CBHW021320160726
47994CB00004B/1534